Meet

Benjamin Franklin

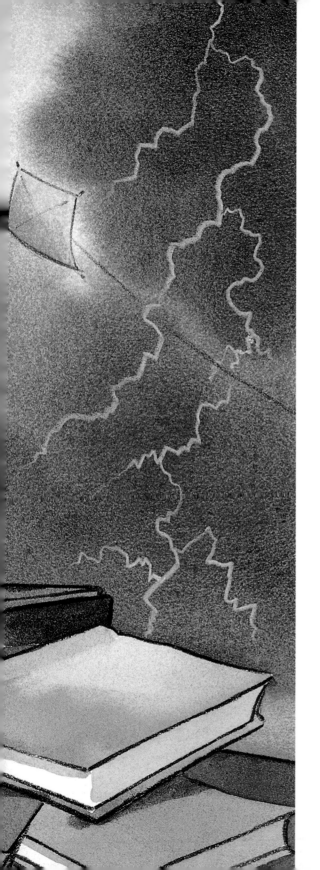

Meet

Benjamin Franklin

by Patricia A. Pingry

Illustrated by Stephanie McFetridge Britt

ideals children's books™

Nashville, Tennessee

ISBN 0-8249-4133-0

Published by Ideals Children's Books
An imprint of Ideals Publications
A division of Guideposts
535 Metroplex Drive, Suite 250
Nashville, Tennessee 37211

Printed and bound in Mexico by RR Donnelley & Sons

Color scans by Precision Color Graphics, Franklin, Wisconsin

Library of Congress Cataloging-in-Publication Data

Pingry, Patricia.
    Meet Benjamin Franklin / by Patricia A. Pingry ; illustrated by
Stephanie McFetridge Britt.
        p. cm.
    Summary: An introduction to the life of Benjamin Franklin that details
his childhood, inventions, and efforts to bring freedom to our country,
and highlights his life-long love of reading.
    ISBN 0-8249-4133-0 (alk. paper)
1.   Franklin, Benjamin, 1706-1790--Juvenile literature. 2. Statesmen--
United States--Biography--Juvenile literature. 3. Scientists--United
States--Biography--Juvenile literature. 4. Inventors--United States--
Biography--Juvenile literature. 5. Printers--United States--Biography--
Juvenile literature. [1. Franklin, Benjamin, 1706-1790. 2. Statesmen. 3.
Scientists. 4. Inventors. 5. Printers.] I. Britt, Stephanie, ill. II. Title.
    E302.6.F8 P74 2001
      973.3'092--dc21
                                        2001006878

10 9 8 7 6 5 4 3 2 1

Designed by Eve DeGrie

Thank you to Dorothy Twohig, Editor-in-Chief Emeritus,
The Papers of George Washington, University of Virginia,
for reading this manuscript and offering her comments.

For Benjamin

From **Poor Richard's Almanack** by Benjamin Franklin

Early to bed, and early to rise, makes a man healthy, wealthy, and wise.

Haste makes waste.

Lost time is never found again.

For want of a nail, the shoe is lost,
For want of a shoe, the horse is lost.
For want of a horse, the rider is lost.

Eat to live; not live to eat.

He that lies down with dogs, shall rise up with fleas.

A father's a treasure; a brother's a comfort; a friend is both.

Light purse, heavy heart.

Great talkers, little doers.

Great spenders are bad lenders.

Sloth and silence are a fool's virtues.

No gains without pains.

To err is human; to repent divine.

Fish and visitors stink after three days.

January 6 was a cold and icy day in Boston, Massachusetts, in 1706. Josiah Franklin came out of his house carrying a small bundle tightly wrapped in a woolen blanket. Josiah hurried across Milk Street and went in the door of South Meeting House.

"**Good afternoon, Josiah,**" said the parson. "**So, Abiah had the baby.**"

"**Yes, Reverend,**" said Josiah. "**My twenty-third child and tenth son was born just a few minutes ago. I'd like you to baptize him. We'll call him Benjamin.**"

"**Benjamin Franklin,**" said the parson. "**Let us pray that Ben will be of use to his fellow man.**"

When Ben was only three years old, his mother taught him to read.

He later wrote,

"I do not remember when I could not read."

But Ben had few books to read. There were no libraries in Boston or anywhere in America's thirteen colonies owned by England. Rich people ordered books from England. But Ben's father wasn't rich.

So young Ben read the Bible. When he came to the last page, he started at the beginning again.

Because Ben loved to read, his father thought his son should be a preacher. He sent Ben to school when he was eight years old. He was the smartest boy in class. (Girls didn't go to school.) In the middle of the year, Ben was promoted to the next school level.

But after two years, his father said to him,

"Ben, I don't have enough money to send you to school. It's time for you to help me in the candle shop."

Ben and his family lived over the candle shop. His

father sold many candles because candlelight was the

only light people had.

Ben cut wicks for the candles.

He filled molds with melted tallow.

He sold candles to customers.

He ran errands for his dad.

Ben hated working in the candle shop. What Ben

loved was the sea.

Josiah was afraid that Ben might run away to become a sailor. He asked

Ben's older brother James if he could use Ben in his printing shop.

Josiah signed a contract making twelve-year-old Ben an apprentice to

his brother James. Ben would have to work for James for nine years.

Ben set the lead type for each word of the newspaper. He read the stories to make sure each word was correct. He suggested better ways to say things. Ben did a good job.

Ben liked to write. He wrote articles and slipped them under the door of the print shop. He signed them "Silence Dogood" so that James would not know who wrote them. James thought they were so good that he printed them.

Ben lived with James and ate his food.

One day, Ben had an idea. **"James,"** he said, **"if you give me half the money you spend on my food, I'll take care of myself."**

James agreed. He thought he could save some money on Ben.

To save money, Ben slept in the print shop. He spent half of his money on food and used the rest to buy books.

Ben also borrowed books from a rich friend who owned many books. Ben often stayed up all night reading.

Ben had taught himself to swim. Most people in Boston did not know how to swim. If they fell into the water, they drowned. Ben taught his friends to swim too. Then if they fell into the water, they would not drown.

Ben liked to experiment with science. One hot summer day, he was flying a kite close to a pond. He took off his clothes and went for a swim in the pond, but he held on to the string of the kite. Ben lay on his back in the water and the kite pulled him all across the pond.

When Ben was much older, he flew a kite in a thunderstorm.

He tied a key to the kite. Lightning struck the kite, and Ben proved

that lightning was electricity.

After Ben had worked for James for two years, he wanted to leave. He liked printing, but he didn't like that his brother treated him harshly. Ben decided to run away.

Ben sold some of his books. With money from the books and money he had saved, Ben bought a ticket on a ship to New York. After a short time, Ben heard that there were more jobs with printers in Philadelphia. So Ben bought the cheapest ticket for a boat going to Philadelphia.

When Ben reached Philadelphia, he was seventeen years old. He had one dollar and one shilling in his pocket. He paid the owner of the boat the shilling.

In Philadelphia, Ben was a funny sight. He had stuffed his underwear and shirts in his pockets. He was tired, dirty, and very, very hungry. He went into a bakery.

"I'll take as much bread as you sell for three pennies," said Ben.

The baker handed him three loaves of bread! Ben put a loaf under each arm and ate the third while he walked around town. Ben gave the other two loaves to a hungry mother and her child.

Ben soon found work as a printer. He saved his money, bought a print shop, and started his own newspaper. Ben never printed anything that would hurt another person.

Ben married Debbie Reed and had a son and a daughter. When Ben was forty-two, he had saved enough money that he could spend his time helping others.

Ben still loved books and set aside time each day to read. He wanted other people to be able to read books too. So he began the first lending library in America.

Ben looked for other ways to help his city. He began Philadelphia's first volunteer fire department. He became postmaster general and looked for faster ways to deliver mail.

He invented lightning rods so buildings would not burn down. He developed a stove that gave more heat than a fireplace.

In 1757, Pennsylvania sent Ben to England to represent the state at court. He returned home in 1762. But in 1764, Pennsylvania sent Ben back to England to try to get the Stamp Act repealed. This act unfairly taxed the colonies. Ben was successful in getting the act repealed.

In 1775, Ben sailed for home. He was sixty-nine years old, but America still needed him.

Ben joined with other men to draw up the Declaration of Independence. They knew this would mean war with England. Ben also knew that if he signed the Declaration and America lost the war, he might be hanged. Ben signed the Declaration of Independence anyway. It was the right thing to do.

In 1776, America sent Ben to France to ask the French for help in the war with

England. The French loved Ben and called him *Cher Papa*. The French said they

would help America.

Ben was still inventing. When he needed eyeglasses, he used one pair to read.

Then he used another to help him see distances. Ben kept forgetting where he left

his reading glasses, so he invented bifocals. This was one pair of glasses for reading and for seeing distance. Then he only needed to remember to put them on his nose.

Ben helped write the 1783 Treaty of Paris that ended the American Revolutionary War. Now there was peace between America and England, and Ben's work in France was finished.

In 1785, Ben came home. Bands played when he stepped off the ship. A crowd greeted him. Ben was seventy-nine years old, but his country still needed him.

Ben was elected president of the state of Pennsylvania and delegate to the Constitutional Convention. America needed a new government, and in 1787, Ben helped write the Constitution of the United States.

In 1790, Ben died. He was eighty-four years old. People in America and France were very sad. America put his picture on the one-hundred-dollar bill to honor him.

Ben helped America gain her independence. He loved reading
and he loved books. He was a scientist and inventor. But most of
all, Ben loved helping his fellow man.